Project Management

One Sitting ... All Set!

By Richard E. Mako, MA, MLS, PMP

Project Management
One Sitting ... All Set!
By Richard E. Mako, MA, MLS, PMP

Part of the book series - One Sitting ... All Set!
By Richard E. Mako, MA, MLS, PMP

An Imprint of
Mighty Mini Publications

March 2023

Project Management
One Sitting … All Set!

The series, "One Sitting … All Set!" provides books of about  80 pages enabling you to begin your study of a subject in *one sitting.* Quickly you will be *all set* and, on your way, to mastering the subject.

Project Management
One Sitting ... All Set!

Table of

Contents

Project Management
One Sitting ... All Set!

Introduction

Project Management is a large field with many different approaches. It is the accepted way of getting tasks done throughout the modern world. If you want to get something done whether it is small or gargantuan you turn to the science of project management and the skills of a project manager. In fact, while you may have a single project manager at the very top you may have many project managers reporting to the lead project manager. Projects may last for a few months or stretch into many years. If you are amazed at the complexity of a completed task such as new word processing software or a bridge spanning a large river or a skyscraper you can be assured, it was accomplished using project management ideas with a project manager at the helm.

Project Management
One Sitting ... All Set!

Project management is appealing in many ways. Certainly, if you are the kind of person who wants to understand how to accomplish a task and the best way to do it, project management is a subject worth mastering.

Chapter 1 – What is a Project?

A project is a series of tasks with a beginning and an end that has a fixed duration. Projects are distinguished from established and on-going operations. Projects differ in how they are managed in different kinds of organizations such as pharmaceutical companies versus manufacturing.

Project Management
One Sitting ... All Set!

companies. You will hear that a project is a project is a project meaning you should be able to manage a project in the same general way in any organization. However, the truth is you will find distinctive ways to manage depending on the industry. Projects may also differ in how they are managed in different departments within an organization. For example, a project in the accounting department may differ in how it is managed from a project managed in the information technology department.

Project Management
One Sitting ... All Set!

Additional considerations are AGILE Project Management and taking a project management approach to managing ongoing operations in an organization.

Chapter 2 – What is Project Management?

Project Management is everything you do to manage a project. It includes a variety of stages, software, and other analytical tools to assist in managing a project. While the standards of project management according to The Project Management Institute (PMI) have remained constant much has evolved

Project Management
One Sitting ... All Set!

including tools that have been added to assist in managing projects. A good example of this Earned Value Analysis. These tools help in managing the standard parts of a project including Initiating, Planning, Executing, Monitoring, Controlling and Closing.

Initiation

This is the beginning of the project. Here you will get permission to work on the project and get management involvement. You want management to have what is called a "stake" in the project. This will also involve project funding. In most projects you will also

Project Management
One Sitting ... All Set!

have key partners who have a vested interest AKA stake in the project. For example, accounting will want to have an interest in how they interface with a new manufacturing software package. You will at least begin to assemble your team in this phase.

As an Internet consultant in the late 1990s and early 2000s I often had a conference room full of vey talented people including computer programmers, database administrators, website builders, designers and many more dedicated to a project. Managing your team productively will always be your hardest task. Generally, the team divided along the lines of technical and creative people. Interestingly, the technical people often thought they were the most valuable people on the team while the creative people differed thinking they were the most valuable people on the team. However, both the technical people and the creative people agreed that the project manager had absolutely no value.

Keep in mind too that many projects simply use the Initiation phase to explore the viability of the project. Often as the Initiation phase moves forward the project viability is questioned and may lead to abandoning the project. Funding may not be available or funding another project is considered more important. Projects may also be impacted by economic imperatives.

While I was an Internet consultant my company was impacted by the stock market crashing and the destruction of the World Trade Center. In my case my chief client was devastated, and all projects postponed or halted.

As a project manager working for a US State a high-ranking employee embezzled funds and disappeared. The problem was he was management and our chief stakeholder. The project ground to a halt and did not come back for 2 years. The point is projects are the life of any company and will be impacted in the same way the organization is impacted. In another company I for which I managed projects lost 265 million dollars in a single quarter. Almost all projects were either halted or postponed indefinitely.

Planning

Once you complete Initiation you can start Planning the project. Note Initiation and Planning may overlap. You may have developed a general plan for the Initiation phase. This will be a detailed plan of all you are attempting to do. WHAT are you doing? Here you will list tasks. HOW much will it cost? WHO do you need to accomplish the project? WHEN (date) will you start and WHEN (date) will you finish? Of course, all these dates are subject to change.

Executing

In this phase you accomplish what you have described you are to do in Planning. This is the work of the project. You should also expect CHANGE to happen which should be managed by your Change Management Plan. In most cases you will have to seek approval for the changes and to communicate these changes to all interested stake holders.

An interesting question that was asked of me in a project manager job interview was, *"What is more important, Planning or Execution?"* When the question was asked my unspoken reaction to myself was – what a stupid question! I immediately rejected the idea that one section of the project was any more important than the other. Further that one of the sections could stand alone without the other. How could you execute anything unless you planned it? What good I the plan if you fail at executing it. I gave what I thought was an intelligent answer balancing both sections equally. I thought perhaps the question was a test to see if I required a plan to begin. I said that I was not limited by not having a complete plan to begin execution. My boss said I want you to visit a vendor in XYZ city but I don't have the exact address yet, but I need you to start driving to XYZ city. Further, he said I'll call you with the address once I get it but before you arrive in the city. I would be fine starting the trip and then receiving the address information before I arrived. The interviewer was not impressed with my answer. Before the interview was over I asked the interviewer for the correct answer. He said, "execution." I have thought about this question since the interview, asked other people about it and pondered it. The question could be discussed and debated without a satisfactory end.

However I think a seasoned project manager knows how difficult it is to execute the best of plans. Perhaps you too can ponder the answer.

Monitoring

This the way you intend on accomplishing the tasks of e project. For example, you may TRACK the project using Microsoft Project software. You will expect each person working on the project to report how they are progressing on their assigned task every Thursday (end of business day) so you can report progress for the entire project to management (end of business day) on Friday.

Controlling

You may have a separate procedure when tasks are not completed on time and a separate procedure to add tasks as your team progresses. You will also want to have a way to communicate with your team and receive this type of information and communicate it to management.

Risk Management Report

You will undoubtedly want to have a RISK Report that tracks all identified RISKS and what is done to mitigate the RISKS. RIsks can be identified and assigned a level of severity such as Low, Medium, and Severe. Examples of risk include team personal and sick time and very specific risk such as weather or various calamities. Mitigations for sick and personal time might be simply ensuring you have assigned additional staff and for calamity an insurance policy.

One of the first assignments as an Internet consultant was to find out how a particular project was progressing. I was asked to get a snapshot of the project. I reported back that the project was more than $400,000 over budget and more than 3 months late. When I reported this information, I was sure they would say to fix it. It was during the Dotcom boom at the end of the 1990s and my manager just said, "Thank you." I inquired about the significant project overrun and delay and my manager said, "Its okay there is so much money being made by the customer and so much money anticipated by the new website no one cares." In almost any other situation my report would have serious consequences but not during the Dotcom era.

Closing

You must determine what your project looks like when completed. Examples include a building is built or software is created and installed. You may also CLOSE sections of the project as each is completed. In most closings one or more signatures from management will be required agreeing that the project is complete.

Postmortem

You may also close the project by holding

what is often called a "Postmortem." This is a meeting in which project team members openly discuss the project successes and project failures. What did we do right and what could we have done better? This will inform the work on the next project. As a project manager you will reap benefits of promoting an honest and safe environment in the postmortem meeting. If team members feel like they can be honest and express themselves in a safe environment you will have the opportunity to gain insight unavailable anywhere else. Imagine how much you can gain by hearing your team express their sincere and unfiltered opinions about why the project was successful. Can you say that you are the type of person and project manager that promotes this kind of an environment? Of course, your behavior will be impacted by the organization's priorities in these areas.

In many organizations an informal party

Project Management
One Sitting ... All Set!

is thrown at the end of the project and sometimes after each project phase. Depending on the outcome it can be a very happy or somber time.

Chapter 3 – Project Management Plan

Another way to look at a project is through the Project Management Plan. In this plan subjects to promote the success of the project are accurately and succinctly addressed. In the plan you typically include the following.

Project Management
One Sitting ... All Set!

Management Plan

In the Management Plan you address management concerns including scope, schedule, cost, quality, Human Resources concerns, communication, risk, and procurement.

It can at times be difficult to determine who management is. You may examine an organization chart and it may seem obvious to whom you will look as management but later you become informed that there are other managers involved or from whom you will need approval that are not even on the organization chart. You will often hear about a manager or even multiple managers that are supposedly "difficult" to interact with. Naturally there are problem people even in management but you should be grateful to hear this sort of information. First, it may very well be true that the manager is just a difficult person and I not pleasant at all. This will be true in some people whether they are management or not. Consider the information to be a "heads up" and something to keep in mind as you interact with them. Second, it may be that the manager is doing a quality job and prefers to operate at a superior level. I have experienced this far more than the first example. Find out what it is they want and step up and deliver if it is legitimately within scope.

Project Management
One Sitting ... All Set!

Requirements Plan

In the Requirements Plan you stipulate what issues the project was created to solve. What requirements have been identified by all the stakeholders? As a stakeholder management may say they want reports that give them a statistical picture of how the project will result in a series of management reports. Build this into the deliverables.

Requirements Creation, Change and Subtraction

Requirements can be the most challenging part of the project. Everyone has an opinion or a solid belief in what the project should deliver. Who is designated to create a requirement? Who signs off on the final requirements document and any changes to that document? This is not about a person but about who gets their opinion in the requirements documentation and who can change that document whether subtracting, replacing, or adding to the document. It is very important to make sure that requirements are enumerated and tracked.

Subject Matter Experts

As part of the project representing the customer you will want to have designated subject experts who can speak authoritatively about what the customer needs and why they need it. These experts are valuable as formal and informal spokespersons. They will be expected to formally comment through to writing complex reports. Informally they are often valuable to you as the project manager when you need to understand a key element of a project from the stakeholder's perspective. It's "Please tell me why they need this change," one day and "How does that work on another day."

Project Management
One Sitting ... All Set!

Often there are several tiers of requirements associated with dates. Certain requirements will be in Phase 1. Other requirements will be added in Phase 2 and additional requirements for Phase 3.

Change Management Plan

A project is designed to deliver certain results. It is not designed to add results that are not enumerated in the Project Plan. It is not about "over delivering." In the Change Management Plan, it will state how changes are made and managed including who is authorized to make changes. Changes may include removing a task or adding a task. There are all sorts of reasons why a task may be added or removed. During the project it may be found that a task is no longer needed or that a task is now vital to project success. This can be very contentious. Often the customer will want to routinely add all sorts of "bells and whistles" that are discovered as the project progresses. Some of the additions must be added or the project will fail. Others are optional and can be postponed. Changes equal money and cannot be simply folded Into the project. Every change requires a decision.

Do we add this now or can it be added in the next project? What will happen if the change is not added? All changes however small must be documented and approvals sought. The project manager certainly never adds or removes a task to the project plan based on a favor.

Process Improvement Plan

In the Process Improvement Plan all changes to current processes are identified. Current processes are mapped and analyzed. Processes are redesigned. Proposed processes are tested and all new processes are documented and communicated. New processes are implemented, monitored, and optimized.

Project Management
One Sitting … All Set!

As the project progresses project team members will see unique opportunities for changing processes for the better. It can be a great opportunity for efficiency gains for the organization, but each must be debated and considered a change. It is a missed opportunity by the organization when there is an opportunity to become more efficient and it is missed because the organization was unable to make the necessary adjustments.

Communications Management Plan

The Communications Management Plan includes all the many ways the project team expects to communicate. The team may elect to use all sorts of communication mediums including telephone, e-mails, text, fax and much more. It may stipulate that certain documents are communicated in a special way, i.e., reports. It may also limit communication such as contracts be forwarded to the legal department versus

Project Management
One Sitting ... All Set!

FAX. It may also stipulate that all meetings have an agenda and result in creation of minutes and that all documents look like provided templates. This is a practical part pf project management that is often downplayed. All the many team members must be able to communicate. In some cases, equipment and software will have to be purchased. There may also be equipment and software that must be purchased as a part of the project goals. The organization may even see an opportunity to rid itself of a communication method that is antiquated. It can be hard to believe just how valuable Instant Messaging (IM) was in organizations in the early 2000s. Or the many iterations of Word Processing software that organizations endured until standards were in place, i.e., WordPress versus Microsoft WORD or, whole computing platforms such as APPLE versus MICROSOFT.

Project Management
One Sitting ... All Set!

One day not long after a project I managed was completed I was walking through a warehouse and a forklift operator called me over to talk. He now had the ability to communicate via *radio frequency* and a touchpad. He showed me the size of the touchpad and the size of his fingers. His fingers were so large that when he went to strike the touchpad and deliver information to the computer he couldn't help but hit multiple keys at the same time. While this should have been identified in the Communications Plan it was remedied with a much larger touchpad very much like what is used by the elderly on a telephone.

Chapter 4 – What is a Project Manager?

In general, a project has a single project manager assigned to manage the project. In larger projects the Project Manager may have additional project managers responsible for managing parts of the project.

The Project Manager has experience managing this kind of project. The Project

Project Management
One Sitting ... All Set!

Manager understands all the many parts of a project. The Project Manager may have additional skills that qualify them for the management of this project. Management may want the Project Manager to be conversant in engineering or in pharmaceutical manufacturing operations or have a computer programing background. Often organizations will require large projects to be led by a project manager with certain certifications such as PMP (Project Management Professional,) Six Sigma or PRINCE. Management may want the project manager to hold additional certifications for example in Earned Value Analysis.

Project Management
One Sitting ... All Set!

Project Management Office (PMO)

A Project Management Office (PMO) is often a part of an organizations overall approach to project management. Typically, there is a lead or PMO Manager that creates policy and interacts with senior management. Essentially project managers continue to manage assigned projects but do so in ways stipulated by the PMO. This can mean that project management software is all the same meaning that project managers all use Microsoft Project and all project data rolls from individual MP software to an overall umbrella MP which is forwarded to management. There are many software packages that are sold to support PMOs. PMs provide feedback on how well the PMO is perceived and what needs to be tweaked or overhauled to promote efficiency and effectiveness throughout the organization.

Chapter 5 – Project Estimating and Pricing

One of the most difficult and complex parts of a project is how to estimate and price all the many components of a project. Of course, management wants to know, "What will the project cost?" As the project manager you will be responsible for providing and standing by this data.

Project Management
One Sitting ... All Set!

The key development tool for estimating and pricing is the Work Breakdown Schedule (WBS). In the WBS you will create a document that essentially lists every task you expect to perform as a part of the project. You may state – Hire Application Programmers but will have to include the many parts of doing that. This will have to be done for every task in the project.

Work Breakdown Schedule

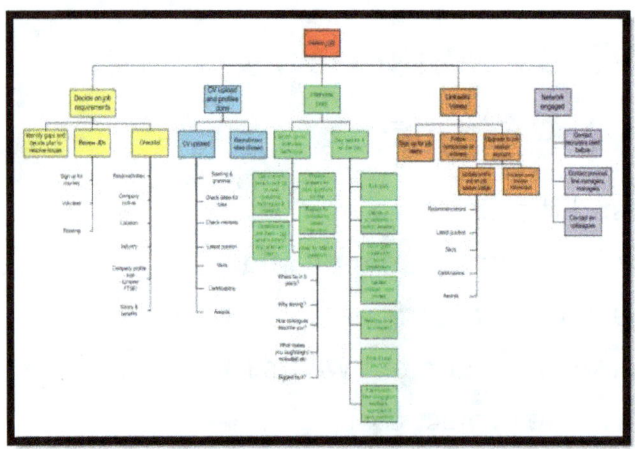

Project Management
One Sitting ... All Set!

The following is an example of what might appear in the WBS for a straightforward task.

1. Hire Application Programmers

    a. Meet with Human Resources to develop a plan.
        i. Place meeting date and time on calendar.
        ii. Produce Agenda for meeting according to template.
        iii. Conduct meeting.
        iv. Produce Meeting Minutes for meeting according to template.

    b. Meet with Human Resources for a job description.
        i. Place meeting date and time on calendar.
        ii. Produce Agenda for meeting according to template.
        iii. Conduct meeting.

        iv. Produce Meeting Minutes for meeting according to template.

   c. Determine status of job description.

        i. Develop a new job description.

        ii. Modify a current job description.

        iii. Approve a final job description.

   d. Meet with Human Resources to determine salary.

        i. Place meeting date and time on calendar.

        ii. Produce Agenda for meeting according to template.

        iii. Conduct meeting.

        iv. Produce Meeting Minutes for meeting according to template.

        v. Assign or modify salary.

      vi. Approve salary.

e. Meet with Human Resources to discuss recruiting.
   i. Place meeting date and time on calendar.
   ii. Produce Agenda for meeting according to template.
   iii. Conduct meeting.
   iv. Produce Meeting Minutes for meeting according to template.
   v. Determine scarcity in marketplace.
   vi. Budget for recruiting fee.
   vii. Budget for advertising fee.
   viii. Determine where to place advertisements.
   ix. Place advertisements.

f. Schedule interviews
    i.   Determine who will conduct preliminary interviews.
    ii.   Schedule preliminary interviews.
    iii. Conduct preliminary interviews.
    iv.   Determine final interviews.
    v.   Determine who will do final interviews.
    vi.   Schedule final interviews.
    vii. Conduct final interviews.
    viii. Recommend who to hire.
    ix.   Extend offer to new hire.
    x.   Gain approval for new hire.
    xi.   Schedule orientation for new hire.
    xii. Include new hire in email lists.

Project Management
One Sitting … All Set!

This is just a small example. The list could get more complicated depending on organization requirements and other factors.

Now for each task you must assign a price and schedule time. Keep in mind many of the tasks will be a part of the overall business of the organization. Human Resources is a part of the company. Management may still want to know these costs. Departments may be able to give you numbers on what their time is worth. Of course, there will be more tangible costs such as cost of advertising and cost of hiring an outside recruiter. I was once in a meeting in which the highest-ranking manager said, "So, we have over 1 million dollars' worth of people sitting in this room. What is so important for all these people to be here?" The manager's point was the salaries of all the people in the meeting room added up to over 1 million dollars. The manager wanted to know what was

Project Management
One Sitting ... All Set!

so important that all of these expensive people had to be in this room at this time and not doing something that might be more productive. The Project Manager should have the answer.

The overall point of this is the importance of the Work Breakdown Schedule. You will often need budget people, subject matter experts and the cooperation of department representatives.

You will need to estimate these costs before execution so you can request a sensible budget. You will also need to track prices so that you can report change and possibly request additional periodic funds. A much better answer when your final price is questioned is that the price of the recruiter rose versus you didn't think a recruiter was need.

On a positive note, this is a good example where you may be able to collapse the schedule based on managing

Project Management
One Sitting ... All Set!

to schedule a single meeting or reducing meeting to save time and money.
Even this relatively simple task is full of possible problems.

-Availability of people for meetings.

(Consider importance of RISK questions such as vacations, sick leave, etc.)
-Availability of meeting rooms
-Gaining access to templates for
  agendas and meeting minutes.
-Costs of an outside recruiter.
-What to do if your ideal candidate
  wants more salary.
-What to do if all candidates are
  unavailable when an offer is
  extended.
-Corporate switch from ZOOM
  to WebEx.

The project Manager and staff (if there is a staff) will present the Project Plan with a Work Breakdown Schedule (WBS) to managers and it will be questioned. The

Project Management
One Sitting ... All Set!

PM must have answers and justification.

Expect to go through iterations.

Chapter 6 – Project Manager Certifications

Different organizations may require different certifications. One organization will insist on a PMP from PMI, and another will emphasize Six Sigma. If the project is installing computer software management may require specific

Project Management
One Sitting ... All Set!

software certification.

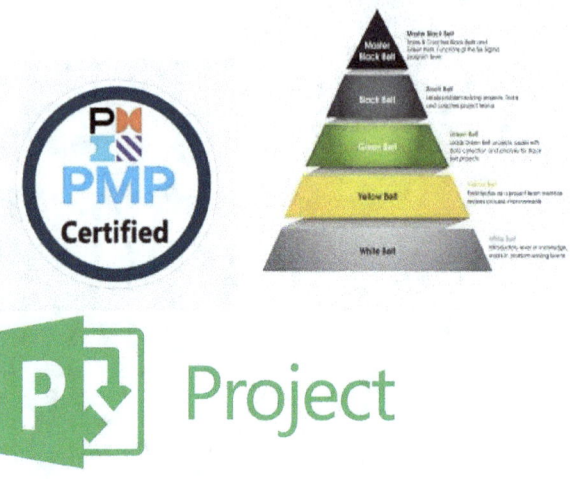

There are also different requirements and emphases depending on the part of the world in which the project is occurring. For example, Europe and Australia prefer PRINCE certification. For additional information please see below.

Project Management
One Sitting ... All Set!

PMI

www.pmi.org

Six Sigma

https://www.simlilearn.com/pgp-lean-six-sigma-certification-training-course

Microsoft

https://learn.microsoft.com/en-us/certifications/

PRINCE2

https://asana.com/resources/prince2-methodology

Certifications can be complicated. When I first looked at PMP certification I thought, "I have been a project manager for a long time. I know how to manage a project." So I went ahead and took the PMP exam and failed. I learned that the exam is not a test of experience. It is project management according to PMI and the Project Management Body of Knowledge (PMBOK.) It is not about all of my wonderful experience but what does PMI say is the way a project should be managed. Later when I took the PMP exam again I passed! You may want to look in the marketplace for organizations that assist in preparing you to take certification exams.

When I took the PMP a second time I asked my management if they would pay any of the costs associated with taking the exam. They said we have no interest in you getting the PMP and like you the way you are. While that was flattering on some level it did not help me with the exam costs!

After I secured the PMP certification I though everyone would welcome me as a holder of the PMP certification. This was not true everywhere I interviewed. If the organization did not have any PMPs they may have been intimidated to hire a PMP. I was asked on an interview, "You are a PMP. You aren't one of those people who are going to endlessly remind us about doing everything by the book are you? Because we don't need anyone like that!" As I said certification can be complicated.

Chapter 7 – How Do I Become a Certified Project Manager?

Different organizations offer different kinds of project management certifications. In the field each has a different reputation. However, this is also true in organizations and even countries.

Project Management
One Sitting … All Set!

In North America, the premier organization for project management certification is the Project Management Institute. They offer many types of certifications with the Project Management Professional (PMP) the most recognized and prized. In fact, PMI offers more than 5o different project management and related certifications.

One of the biggest and most common mistakes in seeking project management certification is to assume just because you have worked as a project manage you will be easily certified. Each project

Project Management
One Sitting ... All Set!

management organization has its own special knowledge base from which test questions are derived. In the PMI organization you will be expected to rely on the Body of Knowledge to answer project management questions. It is not about your expertise honed over decades but about the standards developed by PMI and included in the approved Body of Knowledge. Remember too that the Body of Knowledge is a living document and has changed over time. Also, you may be lulled into a false sense of ease when you hear the tests are multiple choice questions. However, the questions fill an entire screen and are complex.

You should also consider carefully whether getting a certification will help your career. Your organization may like you just the way you are without certification. Also, consider that some organizations may think the way PMPs manage a project is too sophisticated for the organization and its workers to bear.

Project Management
One Sitting … All Set!

Be prepared to study and master the principles and skills the organizations say are necessary to manage a project. There is a large and impressive array of organizations in the marketplace who have developed curriculums and tools to help you (for a price) to pass the PMP and other certification exams.

Chapter 8 – What is Risk?

Risks are the many possible ways the project can fail. You will want to LIST and TRACK all identified risks. In your LIST of RISKS, you want to identify the risk succinctly and include who is responsible for managing the risk, likelihood of the risk occurring, and what mitigation efforts have been identified to limit or eliminate the risk.

Risks include all the many pitfalls that will stand in your way to thwart successfully completing the project on-time and within budget. Risks include the following.

Staff Illness
HR can provide a percentage of employees' illness.

Vacation
Who is eligible for vacation and when are they scheduled to take vacation.

Project Management
One Sitting ... All Set!

I managed a project that was to create and install computer software. The project required expertise from programmers in Norway. I knew Norway used a similar vacation model to what is used throughout Europe. My counterpart in Norway advised me that the shut down for vacation in one of the summer months. I researched how they used their term "Holiday" and discovered that it could mean workers might take anywhere from 6-8 weeks of vacation in the summer. As it turned out all the workers expected to take "Holiday" for 8 weeks straight in July and August. Obviously, this is very different from what American workers do and had to be factored into our schedule!

Work Stoppage
Is a strike eminent or likely?

Contract Negotiation
Is there a union?

Project Management
One Sitting ... All Set!

Is the employee contract up to date?
Who are the union representatives?

Weather

Hurricane
Is the work area prone to hurricanes?

Earthquake
Is the work area prone to earthquakes?

Tornado
Is the work area prone to tornados?

Temperature
Is the work area prone to excessively high or excessively low temperatures?
Is the work area prone to temperature fluctuations that can harm equipment?
Some areas of the United States have weather that can cause risks. Excessive cold does happen in Alaska while excessive heat does happen in Arizona. In some areas work schedules are abbreviated due to weather.

Project Management
One Sitting ... All Set!

Budget Reduction

How reliable are the project funds? What do we do if funds are cut?

Bankruptcy

How solvent is the organization? What do we do if the parent organization declares bankruptcy?

Fire or Flood

What is the likelihood of fire or flood? Are we in a fire or flood zone where fire and/or flood occur frequently? Are fire extinguishers tested periodically and their reliability up to date?

Theft

What is the likelihood of theft? Are we in a crime ridden area? How do we protect project assets? Is everything insured?

Project Management
One Sitting ... All Set!

Risk Identification

Risk identification is limited only by staff creativity. Typically, risks are initially identified in a *brainstorm* meeting and mitigation strategies conceived and acted upon. In periodic meetings over the course of the project new risks identified, additional mitigation strategies assigned, and some risks eliminated. Some risks are easily mitigated with an insurance policy either already in place or newly purchased and other risks tolerated.

The Project Management Institute (PMI) offers risk management certification.

Chapter 9 – What Does a Project Manager Do?

The project manager is responsible for everything about the project. This means that team members and management have a focus point to go to when there are questions, or the project runs into issues that must be solved. There will be different hierarchies depending on the size and complexity of the project.

Project Management
One Sitting ... All Set!

Questions about programming will first

go to the supervisor in that area and manufacturing questions will go first to the supervisor in that area. There will always be questions that arise that are the domain of the project manager such as budgeting, procurement, and communication but even then, questions may be answered by the particular supervisor. Project managers may not know the answer to a programming or manufacturing question, but they should understand the context. It is vital to project success that the project manager embrace what it is the project manager is supposed to be doing. Management will want the PM to accomplish PM responsibilities and not meddle in the details of the work that must be done. So what responsibilities are the domain of the project manager?

1. **<u>Planning and Initiating The Project</u>**

   There is always a time when the only team member is the Project Manager. Typically, the project manager will be hired by management, and they will expect to communicate with the project manager from day one. There will be talk of the vision of the project and how management sees the importance of the project. There will be an initial meeting where a couple people or a room full of people vision-cast and try to provide the scope of the project. Certainly we are not going to accomplish everything in this project so what do we hope to accomplish? What might we postpone for a later project or another simultaneous separately managed project? From these meetings you ill want as goals the scope of the project and the goals of the project. You will want to identify key stakeholders who can be or provide subject experts who can speak to the complexities of what is in place and what is needed. You may also draft a Project Charter that includes what management is giving the okay for the project to start and what kind of a budget will be available.

-Who owns the project?
-What resources will be available?
-When does the project begin/end?
-Why the project is important.
-Where the project will be located?
-What departments will be impacted.

2. ## Resourcing The Project

   The project will need team members to accomplish the project work. Where will they come from? Can they be removed from established units within the organization, or must we turn to the consultants?

   All project staffing will require the project manager to have a relationship with Human Resources. Job Descriptions may have to be written, salaries computed, and ads placed.
   Current workers in departments may be assigned to the project. This may be FT or PT. Percentage of time allocated to the project may have to be negotiated with the employee and manager.

3. ## Ensuring the Team Has What It Needs

   Often equipment and software are

required for the project. Depending on the size of the project and the number of team members all sorts of equipment and software may need to be purchased. The project manager will have to have strong relationships with accounting and purchasing to ensure equipment is efficiently purchased. Who will purchase it? Often the Project Manager does the actual purchasing but must adhere to rules and regulations such as at least 3 vendors must be included in any proposed purchase.

In a project I managed the organization took great pride in being very aggressive in its purchasing and contract negotiations. This resulted in less-than-ideal relationships between the project manager and the vendors. Vendors were so traumatized after initial negotiations there was nothing left on the table. This meant they were not amenable to any change. As it turned out some training was also needed but not in the contract and the vendor now saw its opportunity to recoup what it felt it lost or was unable to capitalize on only making it much more difficult to negotiate.

4. **Solving Problems That Develop**

Problems of many kinds will inevitably develop, and the team will look to the project manager to walk the fine line between the team and any solution. Problems can be identified and then placed on the Risk Assessment List. Here the problem can be addressed and solved or mitigated. This insures the problem will not be lost and give it identification. As in any risk you will want to identify the person that discovered the problem as well as the person responsible for providing its solution or mitigation. You can also add to that a timeframe for when a solution is expected. It can then be tracked through its beginning, any modifications, and solution.

5. **<u>Communicating with Team, Management and Stakeholders</u>**

   Everybody associated with the project must be informed of project developments. Is the project on-time? In budget? What changes have been identified, pending, and approved? What team members are gone or added? There is a lot of truth in the statement that you can't overcommunicate.

6. **<u>Motivating The Team, Stakeholders and Management</u>**

   This responsibility is easily forgotten or neglected. Some organizations provide a budget for a party in the beginning and end of the project as well as a party after each phase. While this may sound extravagant it can be a vital tool to build relationships and celebrate successes. Of course, not every party has to include caviar, shrimp, and lobster! It is a signpost with sincere meaning and a thank you to all team members for a job well-done. If all you can do is gather the team and say thank you don't neglect to do that!

Chapter 10 – Project Management Software

Project Management software is an integral tool for managing a project. Obviously, this becomes even more important when the project is large. It can also be important when the project is spread across multiple geographic locations.

Project Management
One Sitting ... All Set!

The world of PM software is large and diverse. Your choice like any software choice will require a sophisticated list of requirements based on your organization's needs. Primary considerations will be the size of your organization and software cost. Always a concern is opensource or not.

There are four types of project management software, and you will have to examine closely the one that best fits your organization.

Individual

This may also be installed on several

computers and information provided that fits the organization unit.

Collaborative

This software is fitting for an organization with many users involved and multiple stakeholders.

Integrated

This software fits an environment in which there are multiple projects as well as multiple users and stakeholders.

Cloud Based

These fit well with projects that are geographically diverse. Employees may be anywhere in the world. Users only need have an Internet link.

Project Management software can be abused by the project manager and can be a nightmare for the users. Often the software will have for example a feature that enables the project manager to e-mail project members who have responsibility for one or more tasks. Once the due date passes for a task the project manager can opt to have the software generate an e-mail reminder for the task notifying the person or team responsible that the due date has passed. Often the software will also allow the project manager to generate an e-mail 10 days prior to the due date and then 5 days before the due date and then every day the task remains incomplete. Imagine an organization environment in which a project member has multiple tasks reporting incomplete. How many days will the project manager allow the system to keep generating e-mails? This excellent feature for reminding responsible persons that one or more tasks is overdue can easily become a bludgeoning tool creating more and resentment. A wise project manager will use all available tools and will understand the impact of excessive e-mails.

Project Management
One Sitting … All Set!

An interesting experience I had was based on the use of the word "still." I was managing a large project with 10 team members on my team and another 8 team members from the various departments impacted by the project. One of the team members from a department took a particular interest in the word "still." We reported different status for tasks. One of my associate project managers frequently used the word still to describe status with the number of days showing incomplete. The PM said, "Task 100 is *still* incomplete." The employee responsible for that task questioned the use of the word "still" stating it conveyed more than status such as perhaps it should have been completed or for some poor reason remained incomplete. They continued stating there were often legitimate reasons for the task due date to be tardy. Some will say there will always be reasons for the task being incomplete with good or poor reasons associated.

Project Management
One Sitting ... All Set!

We did modify the reporting trying to remove any value judgement associated with a particular task. We simply stated due dates and number of days from the due date to the current date.

Chapter 11 – AGILE Project Management

Historically project management used a "waterfall" approach to managing projects. This means the progress of a project is linear. You accomplish the project phases such as Initiation, Planning, etc. one after the other. This can result in completing the project on-time, within budget but with complete

Project Management
One Sitting ... All Set!

obsolescence or at least partially obsolete.

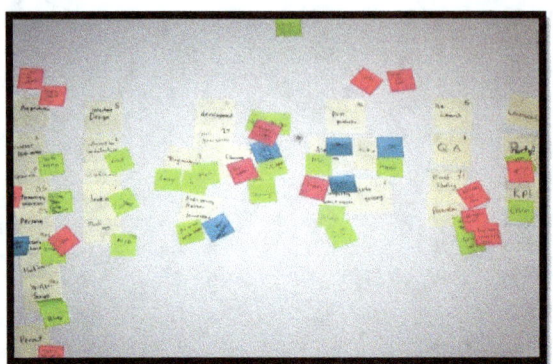

AGILE Project Management progress never stops and is continuous. While there are many varieties of development most have as an initial goal to get up and running as soon as possible with a system that works and then simply refine that system repeatedly. Think in terms of cyclical development. Generally, you will begin with a prototype and then refine the prototype over and over. At some point the system will have enough features to replace the current system. An important concept in AGILE project development is the SCRUM. In the

Project Management
One Sitting ... All Set!

SCRUM teams meet and decide what they will accomplish in key periods of time even for as little as the day ahead. In this way there is continuous development and enhancement. So, while in the waterfall approach you can fall behind in the newest ways of operating in AGILE development you are continually adding to what you have with the newest and best developments. The AGILE approach is very popular in Information Technology projects. For more information see

www.agilealliance.org

Appendix

Project Management
One Sitting ... All Set!

Project Management
One Sitting ... All Set!

Project Management
One Sitting ... All Set!

Project Management
One Sitting ... All Set!

Biography

Richard Mako spent decades honing his skills in project management. He managed small and big projects before and after he became a PMP. He managed projects in a variety of different organizations in both the public and private sectors. He managed projects using the waterfall method and within an AGILE environment. He has industry expertise in banking, manufacturing, media, and consulting. His expertise extends from management of all the expected phases o project management to the sensible and practical. Mr. Mako lives in Southern Connecticut with his wife, 3 demanding Corgi dogs and 2 fussy cats.

Project Management
One Sitting ... All Set!

By Richard E. Mako, MA, MLS, PMP

Part of the book series -
One Sitting ... All Set!

By Richard E. Mako, MA, MLS, PMP

An Imprint of
Mighty Mini Publications

March 2023